UNDER
CONSTRUCTION

Kenyatta,

May this Be
A Hammer for
your spiritual tool Belt!
I Am proud of the man
that you have Become.

UNDER
CONSTRUCTION

7 Things You Should Know
To Build A Better You

RAY SORRELL

purposely
created
PUBLISHING

ISBN (ebook): 978-1-945558-15-3
ISBN (paperback): 978-1-945558-14-6

To those who rest in misery~

If you have ever been confused,

If you have ever been abused,

If life has ever kicked you while you
were down,

This book is dedicated to you.

There are too many names that have blessed
my life to pick out just one.

You know who you are.

Thank you for the love.

◆◆◆◆◆◆◆ Table of Contents ◆◆◆◆◆◆◆

Construction Zone

> *Unless the LORD builds the house, They labor in vain who build it; Unless the LORD guards the city, The watchman stays awake in vain.*
>
> Psalms 127:1 (NKJV)

There are times when I will drive past a new area of town and look at the buildings that are being erected. I will park and watch, for hours at a time, the men in uniforms as they go about their work. The construction sites are usually marked off by rope or tape to warn people that they are in a dangerous area. Each of the workers seem to have an assigned task. Someone may be in charge of driving a bulldozer while someone else may be in charge of the pallet jacks. If you look closer, there will always be someone just standing around waiting for a person to finish their task so they can then begin to work on their assigned area. It is an interesting thing to watch.

After I have watched them for some time, I leave and make it a point to come back. Usually after a few months, I go past that construction site again, and I am amazed at what I see. Most of the time, the area is no longer covered with dirt and debris. The building is no longer looking dilapidated and unsound. It is usually painted and may have signs telling you what type of business it is going to be. The architect and planners have already left, and even the construction workers have all moved on to their next projects.

The reason I love seeing this process of a building coming from almost ruins to a great edifice is because it is symbolic of the growth of a Christian. The Bible is filled with stories of the construction of human beings. Most of the time, when we hear these stories in our Sunday school classes or Bible studies, we miss the building process. Too many times we listen to the lessons, but we forget that those people were becoming better humans for the Kingdom right in front of our eyes. The assembly or creation of the human spirit is a complicated affair that is happening to each one of us on a daily basis.

As we inhale and exhale the air that God allows us to breathe, each breath has a lesson attached to it. Each experience is a brick attached to a beautiful building that God Himself is erecting for the world to see. Sometimes we are so busy dealing with life and its day-to-days that we miss the fact that life in itself is a dangerous construction zone. War, murder, heartbreak, betrayal, love, pain, happiness, disappointment, etc., are all bricks and wood used to build who we are. No person is born a great edifice. We are all living in construction zones, and God is the architect!

The above scripture says that the Lord builds the house, but someone else is doing the labor. God has a great blueprint set for our lives, but it's a process. We must be willing to do some work and get our hands dirty at times. Each brick, nail, slab of concrete, piece of scrap metal, speck of dirt, and brush of paint has been taken into account by the architect. This is also true in creating a better you. God is a master builder and has taken into account every single moment that we experience to transform us to be who He has designed us to be.

This book is not meant to be exhaustive or an all-inclusive fix-it manual for your life; however, it is a hammer, a nail, or a spiritual tool belt to assist you as you walk through your personal construction zone. Let's walk together as we attempt to build a better you.

Ray

You Are Wanted

*Then the word of the Lord came to me, saying:
"Before I formed you in the womb I knew you; Before
you were born I sanctified you; I ordained you a
prophet to the nations." Then said I:
"Ah, Lord God! Behold, I cannot speak, for I am a
youth." But the Lord said to me: "Do not say,
'I am a youth,' For you shall go to all to whom
I send you, And whatever I command you, you
shall speak. Do not be afraid of their faces,
For I am with you to deliver you," says the Lord.
Then the Lord put forth His hand and touched my
mouth, and the Lord said to me: "Behold, I have put
My words in your mouth.*

*See, I have this day set you over the nations and over
the kingdoms, To root out and to pull down,
To destroy and to throw down,
To build and to plant."*

Jeremiah 1:4-10

You Have Been Chosen

If we are to be honest from the start, we all like to be chosen. It really does not matter your age or your stage in life—you want to be chosen. To be chosen by a member of the opposite sex or by the leader of a group or project is a compliment. This is the fuel that ignites our self-esteem and makes us feel special. This shows the people around us that we are special, important, and significant. One definition of chosen is "to be selected because one is the most appropriate to complete a particular task." I like this definition best because it cuts to the chase and reveals the substratum of the divine text above.

God the Father is introducing Himself to Jeremiah, a young Jewish boy, at a time when the people feel like God has forgotten about them. He tells the boy that He already knows him. On the surface, this may seem strange, because there is no indication that young Jeremiah has been to a particular church or worship service. Unlike other texts outlined in the Bible, Jeremiah's background is unfamiliar to the readers, but it is clear that God knows him. God states very clearly that He has known Jeremiah longer than his own parents. He says that before

He formed him in his mother's belly, He already had a relationship with him. This is hard for most people to grasp because we often base our relationships on time spent with one another.

We forget that God is not absent from us at any time in our lives—even before our conception. Psalms 139:8 states, "If I ascend up into heaven, thou art there: if I make my bed in hell, behold, thou art there" (KJV). This means that the God of Heaven is not ignorant to the world in which He created; in short, He is everywhere. There is no surprising God. When He decides to choose a person to do something, He already knows the architectural design of the person that is chosen. He also knows all of the bumps and bruises, or tendencies, of that individual. Please note that this is a foundational importance in your building process. It can also be a scary event in our lives. Why is that?

Being chosen causes trepidation in a dilapidated soul because we know our shortcomings. We know our secret habits and the places we like to visit at dark hours. We are familiar with the negative vibes that we unleash on the people around us. We are familiar with the lies that we have told. We know the hypocritical roles that we play in different circles, so that has led us to the conclusion that surely God has made a mistake.

There cannot be a certainty that for once, the God who controls the universe has finally messed up and picked the wrong person. How could He choose that drug dealer, that prostitute, that womanizer, that con man, or even that killer to do such a divine and awesome work? We say to ourselves, don't worry God, I won't tell anyone that you got it wrong this time. We say we will keep it a secret and hide it in the archives of our mind, but deep down inside we know that this is not possible. We know that God is perfect and does not make any mistakes. But you? Shaking your head, you try to walk away just like Jeremiah. You try to run from your obvious destiny into a secret place where no one knows you. You travel in crowds where you can blend like paint on a canvas, but there is something that eats at you. Day and night it nips away at your core, and you cannot explain it to any of the people around you. They would not understand it anyway. This is because God has already made up His mind to use you. It is already settled in heaven, and no matter how far you try to run, there is no escaping what you were designed to do and be.

Excuses Won't Work

It is interesting how Jeremiah approaches God. He first says, "Lord God." This is an important statement in this text that cannot be overlooked. He is recognizing who the Being is that is talking to him. If it were his parents or some religious zealot, one could understand his next statement. Sometimes we have people in our lives that try to push the envelope and make us submit to their wills. We all have had someone like a coach or a teacher who believed in us more than we believed in ourselves. They may mean well, but their influence and confidence in us are usually met with great resistance. Their atta-boys and you can do its are drowned out by two of the biggest enemies of success: fear and doubt. These cancerous twins have left many people drowning in a river of uncertainty instead of swimming in an ocean of assurance.

This lackluster trust is rooted in relational and traditional fears. It is relational because although these motivators are trying to get you to move to a higher place in your life, you do not trust them. Human beings will not trust people who they do not have comfortable relationships with. This bond or alliance will take place over time through numerous events in which one person is building a trust with the other. When true trust is established, invisible walls will begin to be demolished, and relationships will be formed. This is true in business, friendships, partnerships, and even between the congregation and the pulpit. No one will move to climb a mountain unless they first trust their equipment.

The traditional reason for not trusting is because if there is no historical reference in which a person can grasp from, they will not move towards greatness. Just because you came from a particular pedigree does not guarantee success or failure. There are stories to support either argument; however, it is often harder for a person who has no immediate reference in their family or circle to look to for encouragement. When we see someone who looks like us doing something great, it is easier to follow their lead. But more times than not, examples of "stepping out of the box" are not there. This is why so many people feel like being stuck is the norm. They feel that it must be okay to live paycheck to paycheck. It must be okay to not go after that dream they had twenty years ago. It must be God's purpose for them to constantly struggle with abuse, neglect, and negativity because this is God's plan for their life. Right? Absolutely wrong!

> *He who did not spare [even] His own Son,*
> *but gave Him up for us all, how will He not also,*
> *along with Him, graciously give us all things?*
>
> Romans 8:32 (AMP)

A young Jeremiah would already have had these basic principles etched into his brain at this time. This is because as a Jew, he was aware of the goodness and majesty of Yahweh upon his birth. So recognizing who he was talking to is an important part of this text. But then he tries to use excuses to get out of his assignment. He says that because of his age, he cannot speak. But understand that he is speaking as he is stating that his verbiage is not adequate for the assignment.

He tells a God who is all powerful that He has chosen the wrong person. This is a bold thing to do. To tell God that He is making a mistake is like telling your parents that they don't know how to parent. I came from an environment where even if you felt that Mom or Dad was wrong, you still kept your comments and facial expressions to yourself. But this young man is demonstrating his gift of boldness in his dialogue with God.

He says, I am too young to do this task that you want. Many of us have been in a position where God wants us to move in a powerful way, but we make excuses. We say things like:

> I don't have enough education.

> I come from a one-household family.

> I'm only a woman.

> I have a criminal record.

> I don't know all the Bible words like those preachers.

> That task will be too hard.

I don't have enough help.

People will talk about me.

Who am I to do this?

I am afraid!

What excuses do you use?

When we give God excuses, we are telling Him that He is not big enough to accomplish great things in our life. No matter how pretty we try to make our excuses, we are really saying this to God: I hear what You are telling me, but I don't believe You, and I don't want to do it.

Set Apart

The conversation between God and his young understudy is almost comical. He tells God something that is very obvious: his stage in life. We often do that. We feel like we are inadequate, so we put ourselves down. I once heard a powerful pastor say, "The biggest enemy is inner ME." We were created in the image of God, and our words have power to heal, but they also have the power to kill. The master teacher tells the young lad to watch what he is saying. Our tongue is a weapon more lethal than an atomic bomb.

> *But no man can tame the tongue. It is an unruly evil, full of deadly poison. With it we bless our God and Father, and with it we curse men, who have been made in the similitude of God. Out of the same mouth proceed blessing and cursing. My brethren, these things ought not to be so.*
>
> James 3:8-10 (NKJV)

Just as Jeremiah was speaking death into his own life, we often do the same thing. We forget that we were the only creation that God saw important enough to form into His image. This simply means that some of the same attributes that God has, we have also. One of the biggest lies I heard as a child was, "Sticks and stones may break my bones, but words will never hurt me." This is a fallacy from the pits of hell. Many people

14

have been verbally abused their whole lives and cannot properly function in a normal society. Because a person spoke negativity into their lives, their lives are placed in a holding cell, waiting to take flight. But because they believed the bad report from someone, they will never sail through the blue clouds of life. God tells the young man, "Hold up! Don't say that!" He corrects him quickly to remind him that he was made for a purpose and that God don't make junk.

God Knows Your Fears

The elders in the community used to say something to us children: "You can fool some of the people sometimes, but you cannot fool God none of the time." I guess young Jeremiah was never briefed on the infinite wisdom of God. But God, who is not running for a political office, shot an arrow straight through Jeremiah's uncertainty. Without a need to earn political points in the young man's electoral college, God went straight to the source: FEAR. He tells the newly recruited soldier something strange: "Be not afraid of their faces." I can only imagine Jeremiah thinking what most of us would be thinking: "It's not their faces that are bothering me, it is what they will do to me." But the God we serve has already put limits on what the enemy can do to us. Remember,

---

Be sober, be vigilant; because your adversary the devil walks about like a roaring lion, seeking whom he may devour.

1 Peter 5:8

God said, "All right. Go ahead—you can do what you like with him. But mind you, don't kill him.

Job 2:6 (MSG)

In both of these cases, God was allowing the devil to try and put fear into His servants, but the devil had limited power. In 1 Peter, the devil is being referred to as a lion. Most zoologists will confirm that the lion is indeed not the king of the jungle. He is not the strongest animal, nor is he the most intelligent hunter. A lion's strength is rooted in his ability to put fear into his prey. The sound of his roar can be heard up to five miles away. This verbal threat paralyzes his prey with fear and allows the lion to be perceived as more powerful than he actually is.

In the case with God's servant Job, we often overlook the fact that it was God who brought Job's name into the conversation in chapter 1. This is because God had plans for Job, but these plans had to be first accomplished by the total stripping away of all the things that Job depended on. We will deal with this in a later chapter, but God knew His plans for Job so He instructed the devil that some things he could do, but he could not kill his child.

What we must always keep in the forefront of our hearts is that God only wants the best for us. His way of doing things are so far from our comprehension, it makes us think that God is not on our side, but is in fact against us. It is in His divine greatness that we should always trust. Knowing that once we cross over from living in fear to walking in faith, God is always going to reward us with the next level of opportunity, but we must bury our fear and ride our faith like a wave crashing towards its destiny.

"Precious"

Paraphrased from a guest minister years ago

One day after a nap, an elderly man went to sit on his front porch. As he was adjusting to the heat, he sat on his rocking chair and began to rock back and forth. He looked across the street and saw a young man with something in his hands. He reached into his shirt pocket and put on his eyeglasses. As his eyes adjusted to the new vision, his heart immediately began to sink. The young man had a cage full of birds in his possession. He had a stick, and he was now poking the feathered creatures. It must have given the young lad great joy because he was laughing and smiling the entire time. The older man stood and asked the young man to come to him. The youngster was hesitant, but he finally walked across the street.

"What do you have there young man?"

With great pride, he replied, "I have myself a cage, and it is filled with birds."

"Well," the older man asked, "what are your plans for those birds?"

The lad looked at the cage with an evil grin. "I am going to continue to pull out their feathers. I am going to poke at them until I see their blood. I am also going to watch each and every one of them die."

The older man was touched by love and compassion. He asked, "What can I give you for these birds?"

The young boy's eyes widened, and he answered the man. "Look mister, you don't want these old tore up birds. Most of them cannot even fly anymore."

The old man stood up and said, "I didn't ask you that! What is your price?"

The young boy thought about it for a quick second and then he began to smile. "The price for each bird will be one dollar each."

The old man reached into his pocket without hesitation and paid the price for the birds. He then took the birds to the other side of town. After he climbed the highest hill, he opened the cage. "You are now free birds, because I have paid the price."

A couple of the birds readily exited the cage, but most did not move. The old man then placed his hand in the cage and helped the birds to leave the cage. "You are now free, because I have paid the price."

The story that was told to the church some years ago has a deeper meaning to us today.

Because over two thousand years ago, Jesus asked the devil, "What do you have there Satan?"

"I have a world full of people," Satan answered.

"What are you going to do with them?" Jesus asked.

With a devilish grin, the adversary answered, "I am going to play with them. I am going to change their very nature. I am going to torment them, and I am going to confuse them. I am going to fill their heads with all kinds of evil, and lastly I am going to kill them."

The Messiah was touched with love and compassion. "What can I give you for them?"

With a huge smile, the enemy answered, "The price will be high! It will take You leaving Your heavenly throne, and You will have to go to earth in order to die for them. You will have to endure excruciating pain, embarrassment, humiliation, and even betrayal by the ones You love. But in the end, You will have to die!"

Without any hesitation, Jesus stood to His feet. "It's a deal! Father God, prepare Me a body!"

Jesus loves you so much that He paid the price for your sins over two thousand years ago. He climbed a rugged hill called Golgotha, which translates to "skull." He allowed them to kill Him, but because of this, we are now free. We are free today because Jesus paid the price for each and every one of us. He was pierced in His hands because of our evil touch. He was pierced in His feet because of our evil walk. He allowed thorns to be placed on His head because of our evil thoughts. He was pierced in His side because of the lusts that lie inside of us. But after three days inside of a borrowed tomb, He rose! He rose, so now we are able to rise. We can rise out of any situation that may occur in our lives. When God is on the throne, nothing is impossible.

BUILDING BLOCKS

Answer these questions as honestly as possible:

1. How does it make you feel when someone wants you?

_____

_____

_____

2. Does the feeling of being wanted increase your self-esteem?

_____

_____

3. Has it ever occurred to you that God wants you in His divine family?

_____

_____

4. Do you believe God makes mistakes?

_____

_____

5. What do you believe your purpose is in this
    world?

_____

_____

_____

_____

_____

_____

2

You Must Leave Your Comfort Zone

The Lord had said to Abram, "Go from your country, your people and your father's household to the land I will show you. I will make you into a great nation, and I will bless you; I will make your name great, and you will be a blessing. I will bless those who bless you, and whoever curses you I will curse; and all peoples on earth will be blessed through you."
So Abram went, as the Lord had told him; and Lot went with him. Abram was seventy-five years old when he set out from Harran.

Genesis 12:1-4 (NIV)

What's wrong now?" She looked me in my eyes, and I just could not tell her.

Was it fear, doubt, or just a lack of faith? I really could not answer her, so I just said, "Nothing baby, I'm just excited about a second chance at happiness."

This was going to be our second time going down the aisle, but deep in my heart I knew it was a mistake. Love wasn't the issue. I knew that this woman loved me, and to be honest, I loved her. But just because two people love each other does not mean that they should be married.

My hands were dripping sweat as if I had been working in the heat of the day, but I just couldn't stop this mistake from happening. There was a lump in my throat the size of an infant's fist, and it kept punching me as we made our way to the courthouse to say for better or for worse. The crazy thing was we lied to the same official who married us the first time. The look in her eyes was saying what my heart was saying: RUN.

We walked slowly back to the car, smiling the whole way, and then she hit me with something that never crossed my mind. This beautiful woman asked, "Did you ask God if I am the woman for you?"

My heart sank like the mighty Titanic crashing into an anchored iceberg. Pastor Sorrell, the man who studies his Bible daily, the man who is so hard on others in leadership positions, did not talk to God about this decision. I had been so focused on this fairy tale that speaking to the wisest entity that is known to man did not cross my mind. I looked my new bride in the eyes, and while softly touching her trembling face, said, "Yes sweetie, I did."

Amazing—I moved without even consulting God. How embarrassing is this? Could it be that I was so caught up in what I wanted that I ignored the Holy Spirit that was knocking on my door the whole time? No, not me. I'm a preacher, a pastor, a businessman, a stand-up comedian, a positive role model to a number of people in my community; but also, I'm a flawed and selfish child.

God Will Shake Things Up

My mother, a woman of infinite sagacity, used to always say, "If you want to make God laugh, tell Him what you are going to do." I thought this was somewhat of an oxymoron, because we are all free will beings. I can do what I want when I want. Well, as I have now lived a few more sunsets and a couple more sunrises, I now understand her wisdom. God will shake things up in your life and leave you trying to find your footing. You will feel like you are in a sea-bearing vessel, trying to get your sea legs, but balance will only come when you focus on God.

Can you imagine being Abram—this 75-year-old man? At a time when he should be resting, enjoying retirement, and watching his grandkids play, God said, move! Now allow that to marinate just for a second—move! Not only does God say to proceed in an unknown direction, but He tells him to leave what he knows behind. This would be an alarming event in any of our lives. To venture to the unknown all because God said so takes a huge amount of faith. We are talking about abandoning your comfort zone to go to an unspecified location. During the building process, God will always shake things up in your life.

This is the wonder of being a Christian. To be a child of God means you are no longer in control. You have yielded to something more powerful than yourself. This power is sometimes confusing because we cannot begin to comprehend the *whys* and *hows* of His directions. The prophet Isaiah was reminded of this at the peak of his ministry:

> *"For my thoughts are not your thoughts, neither are your ways my ways," declares the LORD.*
>
> Isaiah 55:8

This elderly Hebrew man was not blessed with the sixty-six books that we call the Bible; he was hearing the voice of God. What an awesome testimony he heard! How many of us would be better off if we listened to the voice of God? Think about that for a second. We hear different voices every day. From the time we rise in the morning to the time we lay down, we are being influenced by someone's voice.

The voice may be a crying child in the next room or a loved one that you know is depending on you. You are still influenced. If we were to be candid and naked at this stage, your influence could be you. What was my influence in marrying a woman when deep inside my heart, I was not prepared to love her as a husband should? That was a scenario that I shared, because just like myself, you have to look deep inside and ask yourself, why? Why do you make the choices that

29

you do? Why do you have the friends that you have? Are your surroundings conducive to growth or destruction? The answers may be painful, but it will also be a great step in growing you to where God will have you.

God Knows What Is Best

Now if what God was telling Abram had no effect on him, the first sentence in verse 2 would have his full attention. God said He was going to make him a great nation. Please do not miss this point: Abram was childless. To be childless at this particular time in history was extremely important. This meant that when the man died, his name and his legacy expired. God was now touching on a core issue that Abram had been longing for in his life. Was it selfish of this man to want a child? Was it wrong for him to want to see a part of himself in another human form? Was it wrong for him to want to give his wife something that was missing in her life?

We all have a void in our lives. This emptiness is something that we often ignore. The reason we act like it's not there is because most of us have either given up on that dream, or our faith has not fully blossomed. We are waiting on a rose, but we have not yet tilled the garden to plant a fertile seed. Some run down the aisles of their local church and figure that if they give their money to the prophet of the week, their dreams will become reality. But the fact is this: until God says yes, your money will not make a difference.

Seventy-five years and now God is speaking to Abram. We do not know if this is their first conversation or their tenth—we can only go by what is recorded in the sacred text—but what we can conclude is this: Abram was listening. There will be times in your life when you are going to have to pause from your agenda and listen. God has great things for each one of His children, but when He is talking, what are you doing? Are you watching reality shows, getting hooked on social media, or being distracted by your own idiosyncrasies? When I was a kid, I heard in church that "God is a gentleman and will not force Himself on a person." I cannot tell you when God is going to open the door to your dream, but He will—especially if that dream is not going to separate you from Him.

Most people underestimate the power of being blessed. The blessings that we receive from above are not meant to be self-serving. God told Abram that he was going to be blessed, but also that he was going to reciprocate that gift. Please do not miss this quick lesson in the law of reciprocity. God gives to Abram, but He tells him that he will also become a blessing to others. Yes, his name, not his title, will be great, but he will have enough left over to give to others. Many people misunderstand this simple rule in giving. When you receive something, this means that you have more than you had previously, which also means that you have enough to share with someone else.

God told Abram this before he even left Haran, and this was a mandate that was etched in this Holy conversation. Yes, we like to receive things from God, but in order to keep them, we must give some things away. I understand that this may not make sense on the surface, but as we dig into the mindset of God, I believe a revelation will occur. God does not ever want to have to compete with anything, including what He gave to you. This was the first commandment that He gave to the children of Israel while they were in the wilderness:

> *You shall have no other gods before Me.*
>
> Exodus 20:3

God Will Protect You

There is a well-known story in my family. When I was about five years old, I was in the mall with my mother. As we were walking around the mall, my mother realized that I was crying. She stopped and looked me in the eyes.

"Why are you crying?" she asked.

"That man stepped on my foot," I told her.

She looked around with the panic of a mother bird protecting her precious egg. I pointed the man out, and by this time, he had walked well past where we were standing.

My mother told my cousin to watch me, and with the speed of a track star, she sprinted towards the man. One would have thought that a starters pistol had been fired, because my protector was in the man's face in no time. She made the man come and apologize to me with the sincerity of a prisoner in front of a parole board. Although my small feet were sore, I was relieved that I was protected.

Now understand, if a mother who is as beautiful as a sunset but also flawed could have a protective instinct for her child, what about God? God assured Abram that He was going to bless the people who blessed him, but He was also going to take care of those who did not. God was giving Abram a guarantee that He had his back. What an awesome God we serve. He was taking care of issues before a problem even came into existence. His blueprint for our lives already includes security.

What we as followers of Jesus Christ need to understand is that He is in the future before the future is presented to us. No one can or will ever catch Him by surprise. Every place our feet land on this earth, God is already there to hold up the ground for our safety. This fact is mind blowing but also settling to the soul. We have a built-in safety net to all the "high wires" we will ever face in life. God will never ask us to move to a place unless He has already prepared it for His children. Now that we understand that God's directions are equipped with an airbag, it's now time to get going.

Get Going

There must have been an excitement inside of Abram because he did not waste any time. Verse 4 says, "So he went." Wait one minute—it does not say that he went around the camp asking for the opinions of his peers. Now please allow me to embellish the text with my sanctified imagination. Abram could have gone to his local church and had prayer with his pastor. He could have watched television and waited on Dr. Phil or Oprah to direct his path; but his orders were already given to him. He did not run to a prayer meeting; he packed his stuff and moved.

> *Trust in the LORD with all your heart,*
> *And lean not on your own understanding; In all*
> *your ways acknowledge Him, And He shall direct*
> *your paths.*
>
> Proverbs 3:5-6 (NKJV)

Now please understand, there is absolutely nothing wrong with asking for help. To be perfectly honest, one should always seek out wisdom from wiser and more experienced people. But I believe that when God speaks to you, you just obey. As long as it lines up with His

Word, move when and as often as He says. Too many leaders have now become overwhelmed trying to be mini-gods to people who should really seek the voice of God for themselves. It may not make any sense to your finite mind, but remember, you serve an infinite God.

Your fire for obeying God will always be a light for others. Expeditiously, the elderly man moved away from his hometown, but he had company. His nephew Lot shows up and follows his uncle's directions. This man decided without even hearing God's voice that he was going to follow Abram. What an exciting time. Before he even left the edges of the city, God's Word was already becoming a reality. As God pointed out earlier, he was becoming a blessing to others.

It is impossible to obey God and not have a positive effect on the people around you. Obedience is like cooking popcorn: the aroma is bound to tickle the nostrils of the people in the next room. Soon they will be salivating to taste what you have. As one pastor put it, "Obedience is contagious." Abram was the catalyst and the spark to ignite the flame inside of Lot. How many people are waiting on you to move? Please understand, a move is not always horizontal; sometimes a move is strictly vertical.

BUILDING BLOCKS

Ask yourself these questions:

1. What book has God told you to write?

    _____

    _____

2. What school have you been wanting to enroll in?

    _____

    _____

3. What person is in need of your spark?

    _____

    _____

4. Why have you been waiting?

_____

_____

5. Does fear play a role in your decision?

_____

_____

6. Are you tired of being afraid?

_____

_____

7. What voice are you listening to, yours or God's?

_____

_____

3

God Is the Architect

"Who are you?" they asked him. Jesus answered,
"What I have told you from the very beginning.

I have much to say about you, much to condemn
you for. The one who sent me, however, is
truthful, and I tell the world only what I have
heard from him." They did not understand that
Jesus was talking to them about the Father. So he
said to them, "When you lift up the Son of Man,
you will know that 'I Am Who I Am'; then you will
know that I do nothing on my own authority, but I
say only what the Father has instructed me to say.
And he who sent me is with me; he has not left me
alone, because I always do what pleases him." Many
who heard Jesus say these things believed in him.

John 8:25-30 (GNT)

Who Are You?

There is a question that plagues the minds of many people today. It is a simple question, but it is also difficult for some to answer clearly. Who are you? I have learned that when interrogated, this query makes many people scratch their head. Who am I? Wait a minute—*who am I?* Some are quick to answer with their position at their job or even their position at the house. They will say things like, I am a construction worker, or I am a clinical psychologist. Others answer this question by saying, I am a mother of three beautiful children. These are not bad answers, but these are not the correct answers. The reason most people get this wrong is because we are rarely confronted with the question of who we are. But for the purpose of this book, ask yourself, what kind of edifice is God building me to be?

We spend so much time in this world trying to be socially accepted and climbing the invisible ladder of success that we lose track of who we are. But to know who we are, we first must understand why we are. Yes, that is the gate to the *who* question. You must know why you are here on this Earth before you can truly understand who you are on this planet. The reason for each one of us being on this earth is to do the will of God the Father. By doing God's will, this makes us His children. Please understand, God was not sad and depressed in heaven, looking for someone to love Him. God is a self-reflecting entity of love and does not need the love of a human to exist. He chooses to love mankind even when our righteousness is like filthy clothes in His sight. If God needed the human race, He would cease at being God.

These religious men had the nerve to ask Jesus who He was. They did not ask in a loving way, but they came at Him with authority like He was a child. They did not realize that they were talking to the *Logos* (translated from Greek to mean *the Word of God*). They were trying to interrogate the Living Word with their own created logic. When asked who He was, Jesus did not hesitate. He told them boldly that He had already answered that question. People will often repeat questions when they do not like the answer that you gave them. But we have to learn to be bold like Christ when confronted with ignorance.

The scriptures are clear—Jesus knew who He was and why He was on earth. His earthly mother, Mary, had to be reminded of this fact. She lost track of young Jesus, but He never lost track of His mission.

> *So when they saw Him, they were amazed; and His mother said to Him, "Son, why have You done this to us? Look, Your father and I have sought You anxiously." And He said to them, "Why did you seek Me? Did you not know that I must be about My Father's business?"*
>
> Luke 2:48-49 (NKJV)

Jesus answered His mother's question with the ease of a gifted child. He said that He must be about "His Father's business." This statement answered the who and the why all in one sentence. He never lost focus as to who His real Father was. So when questioned later by the religious community, His mindset was already established. This will be very important going forward, because you have to know who you are when faced with opposition.

Stay on Mission

As you move in the direction that God sends you, there will be obstacles that you have to overcome. You cannot avoid hurdles in this Christian walk. Barriers and snags will become experience, and experience, when applied, will become wisdom. People are not wise because they have not made mistakes. On the contrary, wisdom is often a surplus of bumps and bruises. This formula is not often shared by some because many are ashamed of their past errors. Instead of thanking God for allowing them to move past that season in their life, some bury those skeletons in a closet marked Do Not Open!

Jesus does not have bones hidden away in a closet, but His focus when faced with naysayers is amazing. He let them know that they were not intimidating Him. He proclaimed in front of the so-called scholars that He was being an earthly megaphone for His Father. He was not afraid, and His boldness could have meant not only social scrutiny but also death. Jesus understood that his mission was bigger than himself, and he was focused on completing his task. You are going to have tenacity and an inner fire like never before. When God called you to do something, He understood and knew all of the pitfalls that would be in your way. There will be times when you will get frustrated, but giving up should never be an option. If you quit, you will become more frustrated later, after you realize that you allowed people who didn't care about you to dictate your future.

Remember, God knows you. God knew you before He called you, and He has equipped you to finish the task at hand. Please know that no successful person has ever reached the mountain of success without traveling through some dry valleys. Those desolate places are going to be your praise reports once you have accomplished your goal. There are always people in church looking at the people who are on fire for God. They sit around and giggle because they do not understand what the people who are shouting have gone through. You must keep an internal bullhorn and blow it at times when opposition comes your way.

Some Will Never Understand

One of my favorite things to do is go to the gym. The competition that I have with myself is sometimes ridiculous. As I have gotten older, I cannot lift nearly as much as I could when I was younger. But there is something inside of me that makes me extremely competitive. Most men understand this drive and determination. But some women would call this silly or just plain dumb. For a man in his forties to try and lift the same weight that he did in high school—well, that may seem a bit irrational. To be unreasonable or illogical for your personal dream, it does not make you crazy; it makes you, you!

Do not anticipate a parade or for the mayor to give you a key to the city. The religious community could not even recognize their Messiah. They were treating Jesus like He was a problem instead of the blessing that He was. They should have been bowing at His feet, but instead, they were trying to trip Him up. It's awesome that the scripture reveals to the readers that they did not understand. Some will simply not understand what you are trying to accomplish. Do not be discouraged. This is actually a sign that you are on the right track.

The enemies of God have lied to God's children. They have sold us a fairy tale that once we give our lives to Jesus, the Christian walk will become easier. This is a lie straight from the pits of hell. Now understand, it is easier in the sense that we know that God has not abandoned us. But the journey becomes difficult because the enemy knows that you are on the path that you were created for. This being the case, he will use every dirty trick to cause you to stumble and fall. The adversary does not want you on the road to glory. His job is the same as it was in the beginning: to kill what God has created.

> *You are the children of your father, the Devil, and you want to follow your father's desires. From the very beginning he was a murderer and has never been on the side of truth, because there is no truth in him. When he tells a lie, he is only doing what is natural to him, because he is a liar and the father of all lies.*
>
> John 8:44 (GNT)

Proof Will Be in the Pudding

Jesus says something that is exciting but also traumatic! He tells them that they will believe what He is saying after He is being crucified. Wait one second—*after* He is nailed to the cross? Yes, some people will not understand your goal or your purpose until after you suffer! It is only after you have had many aches and pains that people will respond to you. What an amazing revelation!

So pain is the precursor to having success in many cases? YES! This is why you must be sold out to what God has for you.

When the pains come into your life, you are on the right track. When tears well up in your eyes day after day, you are on the path to a successful endeavor. When the people who you thought would support you fall away, you are going in the right direction. Remember, God is still the director. We just have to look closely at the script that He gave us to study. No person in the Bible that is associated with earthly greatness comes away without any scars.

You will succeed. You will conquer the mountain that is in front of you. Your faith will be tried, and sometimes it will be tried by fire. But you have a built-in extinguisher called the Holy Spirit. This power that is inside will get you through those days, but know that it will be tears that will fall when you are about to rise to another level. So do not be dismayed when this happens. If Jesus had to feel pain, what makes us any different?

God Is Still Present

My brothers and sisters, please know something that is very important: God is still on His heavenly throne. He has not taken a bathroom break or gone on vacation. God did not go fishing with His buddies. He is not at the golf course. He is sitting on the throne still being God. No person has intimidated God so that He ceased at being Himself. This is important because there will be times when you are going to think that He is not there. Yes, even Christians have moments when we feel like God has abandoned us. We know He is there when things are going well in our lives, but at times of adversity, doubt begins to set in.

This shortcoming of faith is a reality to every person who has confessed Christ as Savior. It does not mean that we do not believe—it just means that we are human. Jesus was bold in His words even after professing that He was going to be lifted up on a cross. Jesus says with divine authority that God the Father has not left Him. He says that because He was sent to do a task, and He trusted in God's direction. It is amazing that Jesus not only trusted the master builder, but He consistently embraced the Father's spiritual blueprint. There was no fear in His stance because He knew that every moment on

48

earth had already been calculated and accounted for by the architect.

Jesus tells these religious men that God is there. He stated something that they seem to have forgotten: God is present. He uses a definitive verb here to express the absolute certainty. He did not say God will be there later. He says that He *is* because He wanted them to know the power that was in their presence. There will be times when we cannot see God, but our faith will erect itself like a mighty fortress. It is necessary in order to quench all the darts that the enemy will throw at you.

> *At all times carry faith as a shield; for with it you will be able to put out all the burning arrows shot by the Evil One.*
>
> Ephesians 6:16

People Will Come on Board

As you move towards your goals and ultimately your destiny, people will begin to get on board. It is an interesting fact that after hard work has been accomplished to build a foundation, then you can bring others with you. The scripture states that as the Messiah was speaking, His words moved people to believe. Jesus was not afraid to stand up to His doubters, and this gave others confidence in Him. You have to believe in you before anyone else will believe. How can you ask a person to have faith in your dreams if you don't have faith in your aspirations? You must become a thermostat of optimism and not a thermometer of uncertainty.

Some people will only climb a mountain after they see that it is safe. No sane person can fault them for being careful with their lives. But there are others who see a mountain as a life challenge and put on climbing boots with no hesitation. The peaks and massifs are seen as a fulfillment to their dull and boring day. For adventurously inclined people, walking on paved concrete is simply tedious. Now some may look at them as being crazy, but we admire the pictures taken from breathtaking places on earth. Their courage at times ignites the flame inside of others to travel to the unknown. You will be a catalyst and propulsion to others, but know that God is still the designer of this beautiful building that is constantly being erected.

BUILDING BLOCKS

Take a moment and answer these questions:

1. Have you ever built or created something
    from scratch? (e.g., a birdhouse, meal, sling
    shot, etc.)

    _____

    _____

2. Were you surprised by the outcome?

    _____

    _____

3. Was there a sense of pride when you created
    it?

    _____

    _____

4. Do you believe that God was proud when He created you?

_____

_____

5. Do you feel that God still smiles when He thinks of you?

_____

_____

6. Why did you answer question #5 the way that you did?

_____

_____

Take a moment to pray and thank God for creating a wonderful person like yourself.

4

Mistakes Are Normal

Now Peter sat outside in the courtyard. And a servant girl came to him, saying, "You also were with Jesus of Galilee." But he denied it before them all, saying, "I do not know what you are saying." And when he had gone out to the gateway, another girl saw him and said to those who were there, "This fellow also was with Jesus of Nazareth." But again he denied with an oath, "I do not know the Man!" And a little later those who stood by came up and said to Peter, "Surely you also are one of them, for your speech betrays you." Then he began to curse and swear, saying, "I do not know the Man!" Immediately a rooster crowed. And Peter remembered the word of Jesus who had said to him, "Before the rooster crows, you will deny Me three times." So he went out and wept bitterly.

Matthew 26:69-75 (NKJV)

Tears began to well in Barry's eyes. He tried hard to stop them from breaking through the dam of pride that was normally there for protection. It was hurting him, and it was overwhelming!

"How could I do that again?" he asked, as the first tear deserted its post.

Quickly, he got up from the bed and went into the bathroom. After closing the door, he turned on the light but refused to look in the mirror. After going in front of the church just two short weeks ago and giving his life to Christ, he was cheating on his wife again. His body felt numb as he prayed through a stream of tears.

It felt like a person had placed a huge weight around his neck. How could he face his wife? How could he face himself again? Could he ever walk back into church again? It started out innocently enough, but one thing led to another. They were just supposed to be talking about the business merger. He barely knew this woman, but somehow she helped him break a promise. She knew he was married, but they still rushed to the sheets like two animals in heat.

As he looked in the mirror, he barely recognized himself. He was naked, and sweat was still dripping from his body. The tears, just like his lust, blurred his vision. Wiping away the wetness, he began to pray. "Father God, it's me again! I know I told you that I was going to do right by you, but I am in this position again," he said, as he fell to his knees. "Father, I am so sorry. Please forgive me and help me to not continue to be a stumbling block to the woman in the next room. Please give my wife a heart of forgiveness, Father, because I know she is tired of me."

Standing to his feet, Barry opened the door and slowly walked back into the room to the woman he barely knew. To his surprise, she was on her knees, weeping and praying also.

Good Intentions

I personally believe that most people in life have great values. This does not mean that we are always going to make the right decisions, but we try. It is a troubling thing when our actions go against our core values. I have known men who are great fathers and husbands, but if you cut them off in traffic, they will show you a different side to their character. They will ride up next to you and have their middle finger pointed up toward the heavens for all to see. There are women who will feed the poor and give their last to a hungry neighbor. But these same women will come to a church business meeting with Vaseline and boxing gloves in their purse. On one hand, they are wonderful people, but on the other, it does not seem like they know God. It is as the Apostle Paul said in his letter to Rome:

> *For I do not do the good I want to do, but the evil I do not want to do—this I keep on doing.*
>
> Romans 7:19 (NIV)

It is a struggle to do the right thing. Living in a world where sin is promoted and holiness is looked at as being weak makes it that much harder. When a person walks into your personal space with their hands flailing back and forth, what do you do? Is it really that easy to turn the other cheek when faced with bodily harm? Most will agree that walking away is the correct thing to do, but what do *you* do? Many of our parents used to say to us as children, "Don't embarrass our name." This was a direct threat, because their name meant a lot to them. You were connected to them, and your actions were a direct correlation to how they had raised you.

Peter was now a young disciple who was trying to show his commitment to his Master. He was now following Jesus from afar, trying to be a faithful servant. The rest of the students had long left the scene, but Peter was doing his best to hang in there. He had good intentions, but sometimes life throws you a curve ball. While he was trying to be a faithful student, a young girl pointed him out in front of the whole crowd. The young kids call this being "put on blast," and she was definitely putting Peter in a bad situation. Understand, Jesus was being tormented at this time, and she wanted to put Peter in that same situation. Peter did something that was against his own words: he denied Jesus. Earlier in the day, he was bragging about his loyalty to his Master:

Peter replied, "Even if all fall away on account of you, I never will." "Truly I tell you," Jesus answered, "this very night, before the rooster crows, you will disown me three times." But Peter declared, "Even if I have to die with you, I will never disown you." And all the other disciples said the same.

Matthew 26:33-35

Peter had great intentions, but fear of the people who were against him made him deny Jesus. The interesting thing about this situation is that Jesus already knew that it was going to happen. He had foreseen not just one denial but three. Peter was actually walking into his destiny and he did not even recognize it. No step that we take in this world will catch an omniscient God off guard. This should be a resting place for our spirit when we find ourselves in situations where we have fallen from where we were trying to go.

Readjusted

Peter was now a walking prophesy. Jesus had already said that he was going to act like he did not know his Master, but he decided to readjust himself. He moved to another part of the area in order to see what was going on with Jesus. This is something to be respected, but some things must happen in life. There are some experiences that a person must go through in order for them to be a better person. We all know that Peter was one of Jesus's greatest disciples, but he had to go through this in order for his journey to be complete. Please do not think that there are accidents in life. Every step that we take in this world is already planned out by God. This does not mean that God will force you to do anything. This simply means you understand that He knows each step before it is placed in your mind.

There was a time in my life when I tried to run from God. I figured that if I were to move to a different city, I would not have to do His will. I was foolish and young, but it made sense at the time. While I was in that city, I don't remember a time in my life where I witnessed so strong for the Lord. It seemed that everywhere I went, there was an opportunity to tell someone about the goodness of God. These were just bricks to my sometimes shaky faith in the Master. I can only imagine God sitting in heaven, smiling, and saying, "I already knew you were going to say that." Even though I moved, God was already there before I arrived. I had to go through that season in order to get to the next stage of my life.

Peter had already fulfilled one denial, but he had two more to go. His moving to a different part of the yard was all in God's plan. Another young lady spotted Peter and pointed him out to the crowd. This time Peter took his denial to another level. He said not only did he not know

Jesus, but he swore to it. This is funny, because I can just imagine him raising his right hand like he was in front of a judge in a courtroom. It is amazing how sometimes we have the strength of a bull, but other times we are as weak as a lamb. Although this is disheartening, God is not surprised by our strength.

If you are going to be a powerful weapon for the Lord, get used to lessons. Learn from everything that happens in your life. You are not a freak of nature, and God is still loving you as you make this journey called life. Like Peter, we find ourselves in bad situations, and sometimes we go deeper into the pit. Don't give up and never quit—it's all a part of making you a better Christian.

Here I Go Again

Most theologians or biblical scholars say that it must have been cold outside where Peter was located. The atmosphere was chilling, but the people around him were growing colder also. After a brief period of time, other people started looking at him differently. It is amazing how negativity can become contagious so quickly. He was just there looking at what the religious leaders were doing to his Master. He was not planning a prison break or even a protest—he was just looking. But the people started paying attention to him instead of the illegal trial that was taking place. This is when the trouble started.

The small crowd quickly turned on this young disciple. This time Peter was more radical than he had been before. He denied Jesus with an oath, but he also began to curse. Remember, for over three years, he had been walking with Jesus. He had experienced all types of miracles, and he was part of Jesus's inner circle. When Jesus was transfigured, it was Peter who was there with James and John (Mark 9:2). When they were stuck in a storm, it was Peter who walked on water and went to Jesus (Matthew 14:29). It was also Peter who declared in front of the other disciples that Jesus was indeed the Christ that they had been waiting on (Matthew 16:16). Although all of these things had happened in Peter's life, he was now acting like his surroundings.

The awesome thing about God is that He gave us the Bible so we could take a peek at the growth of His children. Peter was a human with fears and flaws just like the rest of us. He was afraid, and fear was getting the best of him. Many of us have found ourselves in positions where we wish we could go back and have a do-over moment. In this fallen world, there will be times when the flesh will seem to be winning. Please do not think that you are the only person who has felt guilt knock on your door. The thing that should alarm you is if you no longer feel guilty when you do wrong. Sin will forever be present in our lives until God gives us a new heaven and a new earth.

> *Then I saw "a new heaven and a new earth," for the first heaven and the first earth had passed away, and there was no longer any sea. I saw the Holy City, the new Jerusalem, coming down out of heaven from God, prepared as a bride beautifully dressed for her husband.*
>
> Revelations 21:1-2

Just because you have done some great things in the Kingdom, you are not exempt from falling. This is one of the fallacies in the church today. People often lie about their slips and falls in the house of prayer. Instead of being transparent, they often hide behind titles and positions. This is harmful, not only to the person pretending but also to the new converts. They come into church thinking that they have to be perfect, but there is only one perfect person who has walked this earth: Jesus. It also becomes a stumbling block to new believers when they see a person in authority commit a sin.

Notice the response to Peter doing what was already predicted. The rooster did his job and crowed! This was an instant reminder of the words of Jesus, and Peter was overwhelmed with tears. He realized that he had denied Jesus. This man that walked on water was now sinking in tears. He was hurting, and he instantly became his own worst critic. There was no reason to excoriate himself because this denial was part of his spiritual growth. He had been sitting in class all night. He did not understand that this was going to be a mirror for which future Christians would use to examine their own lives.

BUILDING BLOCKS

When you feel like you have disappointed God, ask yourself some important questions:

1. Did I catch God off guard? _____

2. With my actions, did I stop the world from moving? _____

3. What are some ways I can avoid making this mistake again?

_____

_____

4. Has God stopped loving me? _____

5. What did I learn from this decision?

_____

_____

6. Am I a better person now? _____

7. Did I stop loving myself? _____

5

Be Careful Who You Expose Yourself To

So she said to him, "How can you say you love me, when you don't mean it? You've made a fool of me three times, and you still haven't told me what makes you so strong." She kept on asking him, day after day. He got so sick and tired of her nagging him about it that he finally told her the truth.
"My hair has never been cut," he said.
"I have been dedicated to God as a Nazarite from the time I was born. If my hair were cut, I would lose my strength and be as weak as anybody else." When Delilah realized that he had told her the truth, she sent a message to the Philistine kings and said, "Come back just once more. He has told me the truth." Then they came and brought the money with them. Delilah lulled Samson to sleep in her lap and then called a man, who cut off Samson's seven locks of hair. Then she began to torment him, for he had lost his strength."

Judges 16:15-19 (GNT)

As a young man, one of my greatest pastimes was fighting. I hate to admit it, but turning my fists into weapons was actually fun to me. Please understand—this is before young people began to pull out guns because they did not possess the skills of "fisticuffs." Fighting in my neighborhood was a passage into manhood, and the older boys would often act like we were real boxers. They would place us in an imaginary ring and allow us to release our frustrations out on one another.

This battle of young gladiators was a great joy to me. I was not the best fighter, but I would never stop in the middle of a fight. Some would tell me that I "had heart," but the truth was, I loved figuring out the puzzles in a battle. The older person would normally tell us at the beginning of the fight that "no matter what, protect yourself at all times!" This was the fun part of the fight.

When a person was hit in the right place, they would become discombobulated and forget to protect themselves. I would continue to swing my little fists at their body until they surrendered. I was not the quickest, nor was I the strongest in most cases. I just learned the secret to a successful battle: exposure. When a person is exposed, the strongest person can be crippled and easily defeated.

Exposing your weakness to an enemy is a devastating and disastrous thing to do. The issue is that many people are unprotected everyday and don't realize they have muscles but possess no strength. They have semen but no sperm. They will not have the ability to fertilize the egg once it is presented to them, and they will produce no spiritual offspring. We give the enemies our chin in so many occasions and wonder why we are constantly being knocked out when life throws a punch our way.

Open Your Eyes

There are many stories in the Bible that make my mouth drop open at the attitudes of the people. But if I can tell you a secret, Samson is one of my favorite men. He is, without a doubt, the strongest man to ever walk the earth. His physical strength cannot be compared to any other person in the sacred texts or any person who has ever lived. What is amazing is that he forfeited his strength because his pride was bigger than the muscles that were on his body.

By the time we arrive at verse 15, this woman has already proved in more ways than one that she was bad for Samson. She tried to have him assassinated three times, and Samson never felt threatened. The first time she asked him where his strength came from should have been a warning to the young judge. He was so arrogant and prideful that his eyes were wide open, but he had no sight. One would think that this would have caused warning bells to sound and whistles to blow. But can we be honest? We don't see the signs of the enemies right away either. First, let us look closely at the scripture. Delilah asks him where his strength comes from:

> So Delilah said to Samson, "Please tell me what makes you so strong. If someone wanted to tie you up and make you helpless, how could he do it?"
>
> Judges 16:6

If he had been a man that was at the gym everyday or had big muscles, this would have been a silly question. Samson was picked out before his birth to do something wonderful for God and His people (Judges 13:3-5). People will wonder how you are able to do the things that you do. When God has ordained and separated you for a purpose, things that are difficult for others will be simple for you. This is largely due to the framework that God has placed around you to handle the load before you were even a thought in your daddy's brain.

There are people with amazing gifts in the kingdom of God, but those gifts are never developed. We spend so much time trying to please the flesh that we often miss the pure blessings of our gifts. I have witnessed mothers who raised their children on their own and never complained. I have also seen pastors who were wrongfully accused by an entire church and never batted an eye. As a young man, I saw my sister go through a terrible heartbreak, but she never spoke a bad word toward the person who hurt her. These are wonderful gifts of strength, but they are often overlooked in the body of Christ.

God has given His children everything that we need to succeed. Think about your gift. You may be asking, "What is my gift?" A person once told me a simple way of finding your gift. Your gift is the thing that you do best with the least amount of effort. Now think about it—what is your gift?

Have you exposed your gift to the wrong people? Don't worry—most people have made the same mistake.

Watch Your Company

This woman was consistent in her efforts to destroy this man. It is almost humorous that no man could take Samson down, but a woman could with ease. The things in life that we think are not a threat are normally our biggest foes. There is nothing like being betrayed by someone who you have shared intimate moments with. So many people can testify that the spouse they once loved is now their biggest headache.

It is a harsh reality to love a person one day and loathe them the next. After planning a beautiful wedding for months, after being joined together in front of God and family, now you cannot stand the sight of him or her. This man who you used to rush home to is now blocked from every social site that you own. She was your "little Boo Boo," but now if you see her, it's like seeing a ghost. Good company quickly turns into terrible company.

Although Samson's story is different, it is still similar to many of ours. When we really look back at our stories, there are always signs that we ignored. I know, I know—you didn't see it. Well, as a police officer told me when he stopped me for speeding, "Just because you did not see the sign does not mean you won't get this ticket!" Unfortunately, we must pay the fines for the choices in our lives.

Samson should have stopped the offense from the offset. The first time this woman showed her teeth, he should have left quickly. It is hard to leave a place of comfort. It's even harder when you are comfortable with being in an uncomfortable place. Many people go to places that they know is not right for them, but it's their norm. Change is not an option, because that would take effort. Every day, she pressed the issue about his strength. She began to make his comfortable place tense, and he was getting tired of it. The Bible said that she was "getting on his nerves." One would think that this is a perfect opportunity for him to get up and leave, but he stayed. She bothered him so much that his soul was vexed unto death! Wait a minute—but you are still in her presence?

So many people are dealing with dangerous issues every day. Domestic violence is a common thing in the church today. Many people do not talk about their experiences, and this is usually because of embarrassment. After they have made it out of the abuse, shame is an emotion that many people say they felt. It is nothing to be ashamed of; just thank God that He delivered you from that horrible situation. The company that Samson was keeping was breaking him down daily, like a mathematical fraction, and he didn't even see it.

When a person is abusive, the first swing is always stealthy. They may start with words before they get to the physical abuse. This is a test to see how much they can get away with. They are seeing if they go a step further, will there be consequences for their actions? They normally do not start off with a punch to the face. Their abuse is calculated and timed for the next attack. This is why you must watch who you allow to be in your company. Satan will use whatever force he can to break you down and utterly break your heart. He will see the building process taking place in your life, and he will try to place spiritual termites in your life to destroy what God is developing.

Be Careful Who You Give Your Heart To

This is an incredible story of such a powerful man of God who was so weak. In verse 17, it says that he told her his whole heart. This woman, who had showed that she was an enemy and not a friend, was entrusted with this judge's heart. On the surface, it makes no sense, but we must go back in time in order to understand what Samson was dealing with:

Some time later Samson went to visit his wife during the wheat harvest and took her a young goat. He told her father, "I want to go to my wife's room." But he wouldn't let him go in. He told Samson, "I really thought that you hated her, so I gave her to your friend. But her younger sister is prettier, anyway. You can have her, instead." Samson said, "This time I'm not going to be responsible for what I do to the Philistines!" So he went and caught three hundred foxes. Two at a time, he tied their tails together and put torches in the knots. Then he set fire to the torches and turned the foxes loose in the Philistine wheat fields. In this way he burned up not only the wheat that had been harvested but also the wheat that was still in the fields.

> *The olive orchards were also burned. When the*
> *Philistines asked who had done this, they learned*
> *that Samson had done it because his father-in-law,*
> *a man from Timnah, had given Samson's wife to a*
> *friend of Samson's. So the Philistines went and*
> *burned the woman to death and*
> *burned down her father's house.*
>
> Judges 15:1-6

We all have a beginning in our lives. Just because you see a person being a crook or dancing in a strip club, that doesn't mean it's their genesis. Just as words evolve over the years, so do people. Each of us has an origin, but unfortunately, this is not what people focus on. Samson had been severely hurt, and for most of his life, he was rebellious to his own pain. We find in chapter 14 of Judges that he left his bride at the wedding celebration. When he came back to consummate the marriage, he was stopped at the door. He was trying to have intercourse with his wife but was hit with bad news. Her father denied him and then told him that he was no longer the husband.

This is where we see Samson losing his head and begin to make terrible choices. His wife had not only been given away to his friend, but she was now dead because of his actions. We have to understand why we make the decisions that we make. There is always a birth to our choices. The fertilization of our ideas and brainchildren are not absent from a seed. No person wakes up and decides they want to be a drug dealer or a prostitute. It is normally a systematic set of circumstances that leads us to our choices. Society at large does not care about the why; they only focus on the result. This is when judgment of our fellow man comes into play. Instead of being a subpoenaed witness for Jesus, we quickly become a self-appointed judge.

Now that we see Samson's heart being broken, it is easier for us to understand why he stayed with this woman. He had lost before, and he was dead set on not losing again. Even with the person exposing herself, he shared his whole heart. It was not about losing his strength at this stage; he did not want to lose his woman. He made his heart and his feelings more important than his relationship with God. This is something that many of us have done in our own lives. We ask God for a mate, but then we make the new relationship a priority and put God on the back burner.

Too many times we treat God like He is a spare tire. We take Him out of our spiritual trunks when our tires are deflated. Then we return Him to that secret compartment once we have gotten up the road. This is a sad commentary in many of our lives. Instead of sharing our hearts with God, we often give it to a flawed person who will use our secrets against us on "mad day." This is the day that people become angry and shout to the world what you shared with them privately. Be careful who you share your all with. Not everyone who says they love you really does. Some people are heartless and do not mean you well. You must learn to discern who God has placed in your lives and who is there to tear you down.

Your Enemy Is Heartless

After Samson exposed himself, he was wide open for an attack from the enemy. He told his whole heart to Delilah, a proven foe to his peace. This woman was in a relationship strictly for her own interests. Nowhere do we find her showing love to this man, but he trusted her with his deepest secret. Just like a black widow spider, she spun her web, and now, it was time to eat her prey.

After she secured payment for her work, she had one task left. She used her art of seduction and put him to sleep. Many theologians or biblical scholars have tried to explain his deep sleep. Some have said that she slipped him something that would make him drowsy and ultimately sleep, but I am inclined to believe another popular reasoning. She knew that Samson would fall into a deep sleep after having sex with her. But no matter what position you take, it is recorded that he was asleep.

Many people find themselves in a deep sleep from a spiritual perspective. They have dozed off at the wheel while driving the vehicles in their own lives. Instead of enjoying the beautiful views of life, they are on cruise control headed into a brick wall. God never called us to be a footstool for our enemies.

> *The LORD said to my Lord, "Sit at My right hand, Till I make Your enemies Your footstool."*
>
> Psalms 110:1 (NKJV)

This man who killed a thousand Philistines with a jawbone of a donkey defeated himself with his own words (Judges 15:16). Now he is in a deep, coma-like sleep, and she calls for a barber to cut his locks of hair. His sleep had to be deep in order to not feel the dead, keratinized cells being cut from his scalp. I know you may be saying at this point, how could he not feel that? I agree, but this is the trick of our enemy. You will not even know that you are being attacked until it is too late. Your money will be gone. Your family will be destroyed. Your core values will be changed. Your reputation will be executed. Your strength will be ripped from your muscles, and you won't recognize it until it is too late.

WAKE UP! Your enemy is trying to rob all the riches that God has given to you. They use smooth words like *politically correct* and *don't offend* while they are sucking the life out of you. Society accepts the assimilation, so oftentimes, we go along with the program. Before you have time to wake up from the hypnosis, your strength has disappeared! You have lain on the enemy's lap for so long that you don't even recognize yourself any longer. Your eyes look different. Your nose looks different. Your hair has been reduced from shoulder length to looking like you just joined the Marines.

BUILDING BLOCKS

Ask yourself some important questions:

1. Have I exposed myself to the wrong person?

_____

2. What did they do with that important part of me?

_____

_____

3. How did that make me feel?

_____

_____

4. What are some steps that need to be addressed to get my security back?

_____

_____

5. What are my areas of strength?

_____

_____

6. Have I used my gifts for the glory of God?

_____

_____

7. Is God pleased with my utilization of my gifts?

_____

_____

8. Am I helping others find their gifts?

_____

_____

6

You Have to Get Naked

The woman saw how beautiful the tree was and how good its fruit would be to eat, and she thought how wonderful it would be to become wise. So she took some of the fruit and ate it. Then she gave some to her husband, and he also ate it. As soon as they had eaten it, they were given understanding and realized that they were naked; so they sewed fig leaves together and covered themselves. That evening they heard the Lord God walking in the garden, and they hid from him among the trees. But the Lord God called out to the man, "Where are you?" He answered, "I heard you in the garden; I was afraid and hid from you, because I was naked."

Genesis 3:6-10 (GNT)

"This is it," Rob said to himself. The football tryouts had gone well. Most of his friends had played organized sports since the first and second grade. This was not the case for Rob. His mother was a single parent, and they never had money for anything except paying the monthly expenses. He was nervous, but the coach said that he did well for his first time playing football. All summer he anticipated putting on the pads and the colors that represented his school. He was only in the seventh grade, but he felt like he had just entered into the NFL.

There was a smell in the locker room that he couldn't identify. A scent of pride among peers, and he was proud to be a part of this atmosphere. Then the coach stepped out of his office and told the teenagers something that frightened Rob. He yelled loudly in a commanding tone, "Don't forget to shower before you go to your next class!"

Immediately, like a herd of cattle, all the boys started heading towards the shower area. They began to strip off their clothes with no hesitation. Rob was stunned. "What is going on?" he thought to himself. "Am I supposed to get naked and shower next to everyone?" He began to shake at the thought of being nude in front of the other boys.

First Time Seeing You

Many people can relate to the illustration of the first time being naked in front of a stranger. To be completely honest, you can be with a person for years and still be uncomfortable being bare or in your birthday suit. You may not be secure with the parts that God has given you or maybe it is just the unknowing response that you may get. No matter how old you are, this is an issue that many people struggle with. To disrobe or strip down to your God-given rawness is hard in the flesh and may never be a norm for some. To show another human being what lies beyond the fancy name tags and designer labels is a mountain that some may never be able to climb. But what about being naked in the spirit?

So many have given people they love a spiritual lap dance. They only show enough of themselves so they can be loved and adored, but they will never bare their all. It is too intimidating to strip out of your zip codes, your degrees, and your social norms. Showing the world what lies beneath the cloth and materials would take great courage that many of us do not possess. We have been programmed to hide in the compartments of our success and only reveal what is conducive for our comfort. Even in our worship experience, we tease each other but never become naked. When the right song is played, we do a spiritual striptease, but God is not fooled.

BUILDING BLOCKS

Ask yourself some quick questions:

1. Have you ever been spiritually naked?

_____

2. Have you ever bared all that you have before a person?

_____

3. Have you ever been spiritually nude before God?

_____

The sacred text at the beginning of this chapter is interesting because it shows the first time Adam and Eve knew that they were naked. They had been walking around in the nude the whole time, but their eyes were opened through an act of disobedience. God told them not to eat from the tree of knowledge, but they disobeyed His command. It was a decision that opened a can of troubles that they would not be able to close on their own.

> *And the LORD God commanded the man, saying, "Of every tree of the garden you may freely eat; but of the tree of the knowledge of good and evil you shall not eat, for in the day that you eat of it you shall surely die."*
>
> Genesis 2:16-17 (NKJV)

They were now seeing life from a whole different perspective. There will be no more walking in the Garden of Eden, enjoying the cool breeze of the day against their naked parts. They were ashamed of what God made. God said, "It was very good," but they were embarrassed of God's greatest creation: humans (Genesis 1:31). Seeing yourself for the first time can create anxiety and fear in a person's life. Some people have lied to themselves for so long that when their eyes are truly opened, it is like a floodlight being pointed in their direction. The veil is lifted, and all of the perfect imperfections are revealed to the world. The revelation and declaration is that most people have already seen what you may have thought was hidden.

One of the Bible's greatest prophets had to deal with an eye-opening experience. The senior statesman Isaiah was shaken when his eyes saw the Lord sitting on His throne:

In the year that King Uzziah died, I saw the Lord. He was sitting on his throne, high and exalted, and his robe filled the whole Temple. Around him flaming creatures were standing, each of which had six wings. Each creature covered its face with two wings, and its body with two, and used the other two or flying. They were calling out to each other: "Holy, holy, holy! The Lord Almighty is holy! His glory fills the world." The sound of their voices made the foundation of the Temple shake, and the Temple itself became filled with smoke. I said, "There is no hope for me!

> *I am doomed because every word that passes my lips is sinful, and I live among a people whose every word is sinful. And yet, with my own eyes I have seen the King, the Lord Almighty."*
>
> Isaiah 6:1-5 (GNT)

Adam and Eve tried to hide because they were not used to what they were now seeing. Many people try to hide from their realities and live in a state of stealth from the rest of the world. This is something that is common in today's church environment. People will not become spiritually nude out of fear of judgment from others. Adam and Eve hid behind fig leaves, but today, people are more sophisticated with their disguises.

The false fronts people use today are wearing designer labels, driving fancy cars, and working in the tallest buildings in the city. We now conceal the nakedness with church lingo and religious language. As long as you can speak pious protocol and expound ecclesiastical dialects, people will never know how naked you need to be to get a true relationship with God. Too many times we act like Grandpa Adam and Grandma Eve. We hide in the shadows of fear and uncertainty instead of embracing the sunshine of originality and individuality. We are like little children playing make believe and often buy into what we have sold ourselves. But in order to get a closer relationship with God, we must put the fig leaves down. We have to come out of hiding and tell God, "Here I am, naked before you."

Hiding From Your Reality

It is absolutely amazing how many people live in pseudo and imaginary worlds. You and I come into contact with them everyday. Unless you get to know them, you will never notice the fairy tale that they call life. They live in homes that they cannot afford and drive cars that are too expensive, and they are usually drowning in debt. Simply put, they have not accepted their reality. Truth of the matter is, they are living a lie, but they want the world to perceive them in a particular way.

I have learned early in my life that living a lie is a useless act. Why try to impress people who deep down really do not care about you? Life is too short to live that way. But the reason that I came to this conclusion is, God knows the truth. It seems like a silly thing to hide who you really are, but when you think about it, most people do this every day. But how do you hide from God? You can fool the people at the church into thinking you are all that and a bag of chips but not God.

First we have to remember that God is omniscient. This means that there is never a time in our lives that we can fool Him. No matter how much we give to the poor, He knows if we did it from the heart or to be seen. Even if we decide to be at the church every time the doors are open, He knows our motives. If it is based on love, He knows. If our staying at each service is because we are trying to secure a prominent position, He knows that also. So why play the game of make believe? It has more to do with the opinions of others than it does with ourselves. We are often committed to pleasing people rather than pleasing God. But God sees everything.

Adam and Eve tried to hide themselves from the voice of God. They hid from the presence of God. Wait a minute! They didn't want to be in God's presence? All that they knew at this time in their lives was to be in God's company. Think about this for a second: Adam and Even were the only humans to actually be in the direct presence of God. Yes, years later we would be able to *feel* His presence through the gift of the Holy Spirit (John 14:26), but they had direct contact with the King of Kings. Before this act of disobedience, they knew no sin, so they were able to "hang with the Father." Now, they try to hide—from God!

Looking back at this situation, I believe that Adam and Eve would laugh at how silly they were. Playing hide and seek with God is like selling ice to an Eskimo—useless. But they were hiding from their reality. The reality of sin had hit them in the mouth, and they were acting foolishly because of it. Most people, if they were to be candid, can actually relate. We may not hide behind fig leaves, but we camouflage our mistakes just the same.

We need to learn to accept our truth. Years ago, I was fortunate enough to work with some individuals who were attending an alcohol anonymous class. After forming a relationship with them, they allowed me to go to a class with them. The classroom was filled with souls who had experienced all walks of life. At the beginning of each person's testimony, they would each start their story with, "Hello, my name is (fill in the blank), and I am an alcoholic." I was floored because some of these people had not had a drink of alcohol in years. After the meeting, I was told this was done because it was a reminder to themselves that this painful sickness was part of their reality.

God Is Not Fooled

Remember what was told to the children in an earlier chapter: "You can fool some of the people, some of the time. You can fool most of the people, most of the time. But you cannot fool God, none of the time!" As a kid, I used to think this was a logic that was rooted in ignorance. I understood that it was crazy to try to fool God because He knew everything and was everywhere. My small mind could not comprehend a person trying to "get one over" on God. This is why verse 9 is so comical if not looked at through sensitive eyes.

Picture, for the first time in history, a person using their carnal eyes. Up until this point in their lives, Adam and Eve were walking in perfection. They did not even understand what it meant to not only have fear but also guilt. They were hiding from God because they didn't know what else to do. This is what happens to many of us today. When faced with a new burden, oftentimes we react in an irrational way. The first time a teenager's heart is broken, they don't know how to handle it. Some will cry uncontrollably while others retreat to the secret confinement of their rooms. Whichever way they choose to handle it, many will say things like, "get over it," or "it's just puppy love." But to the person who is dealing with this new experience, are they really wrong for dealing with it as they see fit?

The wondrous and magnificent thing about God is He was in chill mode the whole time. Nowhere in the text does it appear that God is stirred by their hiding. He asks a beautiful rhetorical question when He hits the scene: "Adam, where are you?" This is a question that He was already privy to. What God was asking Adam was, what state of mind are you in now? He was not concerned about Adam's location. His concern was about their relationship. Up until now, Adam and Eve could have a face to face with God because sin did not separate them. It is sin that separated God's greatest creation from Himself. Because of their decisions, we can no longer see the face of God. Moses, the first leader of Israel, was reminded of this when he requested to see God's face:

> But He said, "You cannot see My face; for no man shall see Me, and live."
>
> Exodus 33:20 (NKJV)

There are many who believe that even though God knew the fall of man would take place, His heart was still broken. When we go against the grain of God, it has an effect on heaven. Heaven is watching our lives, and even the angels are rooting for us. Jesus was very clear as He spoke to the religious leaders of the community:

> "Suppose one of you has a hundred sheep and loses one of them—what do you do? You leave the other ninety-nine sheep in the pasture and go looking for the one that got lost until you find it. When you find it, you are so happy that you put it on your shoulders and carry it back home. Then you call your friends and neighbors together and say to them, 'I am so happy I found my lost sheep. Let us celebrate!'

> *In the same way, I tell you, there will be more joy in heaven over one sinner who repents than over ninety-nine respectable people who do not need to repent."*
>
> Luke 15:4-7 (GNT)

So now the relationship is broken. God is in the garden talking to His creation from a different place than He was used to speaking to them—at a distance. This is the case today as it was in the garden. When we run from God, it creates an abyss between Creator and creation. Yes, Jesus died and was raised from the dead to repair this damaged relationship, but our rejection of relationship is a choice that we make every day. We choose what we want to be around, but God cannot be around sin. Sin and holiness go together like oil and water—they don't mix. Adam understood this instantly and went into hiding because fear had gripped his soul for the first time in his small existence.

Fear

Adam was now a delirious and fearful soul. He was seeing through sinful eyes for the first time.

It was a shock to his equilibrium, and he retreated behind the thing that he had dominion over. Fear was gripping his mind and body like vice grips attached to metal. It was squeezing his thoughts, and he actually felt like he was hiding. He told God something that was already known to the universe: I'm afraid. Most people will point their finger at Adam for his disobedience, but how do we react when we are afraid?

Someone once said, "Fear is the opposite of faith." It is hard to imagine or even conceptualize what was going on in Adam's mind. He was afraid. The first time in history, a man was using an emotion that was, up to this time, foreign and non-existent to the brain. The encephalon, the brain, was working overtime, and fight or flight was in full effect. He knew that his small arms were too small to box with God, so he retreated behind leaves. He was naked and did not want God to see his exposed parts. Many of us today face the same quandaries and dilemmas. We are naked and ashamed, but God is telling us to come from behind the pseudo shelters. He wants to have a relationship with us, but fear has become a comfortable place of discomfort.

Our lives are a testimony of God's goodness to us but also a statement of our fears. Instead of being naked and proud, we are nervous because we think God cannot handle us this way. We have believed the myth that God only speaks to those in fancy suits and big hats. Some have prescribed to the notion that God doesn't deal in mess, so we think that we must clean ourselves up. This is a lie straight from the pits of hell! God is a loving God who does not mind getting His holy hands dirty. He placed them in the dust in order to make man. Every time you look in the mirror, remember that God is a dirt specialist.

Adam had not only hidden himself, but he was also out of order as it relates to his bride. He was supposed to be a protector and a leader. Due to his disobedience, he had turned into a coward and a follower. His role was compromised and generations that should have taken after his lead will now be punished. The seeds that we plant today will yield a harvest eventually. It is imperative that we make the tomorrows of our lives proud of the choices of today. It's hard at times, but it gets even more difficult as bad choices turn into a destroyed life. You have to make up your mind that you are going to obey God at all costs. This means you must become spiritually naked, vulnerable, and unashamed. Allow God to view you without the fig leaves in our lives. God is waiting and wanting to have a great relationship with you because not only does He deserve it, but so do you.

BUILDING BLOCKS

Take a few moments and answer these questions:

1. Are you ready to be naked before God?

_____

2. What excuses have stopped you in the past?

_____

_____

3. Do you feel like you are unworthy of God's love?

_____

_____

4. Do you think God accepts you?

_____

_____

5. Do you accept you?

_____

_____

6. Was there a point in your life when you felt rejected?

_____

_____

_____

_____

_____

_____

_____

Fight for Your Life

> That same night Jacob got up, took his two
> wives, his two concubines, and his eleven
> children, and crossed the Jabbok River.
> After he had sent them across, he also sent across
> all that he owned, but he stayed behind, alone.
> Then a man came and wrestled with him until just
> before daybreak. When the man saw that he was
> not winning the struggle, he hit Jacob on the hip,
> and it was thrown out of joint. The man said,
> "Let me go; daylight is coming." "I won't, unless you
> bless me," Jacob answered. "What is your name?"
> the man asked. "Jacob," he answered. The man said,
> "Your name will no longer be Jacob. You have
> struggled with God and with men, and you have
> won; so your name will be Israel."
>
> Genesis 32:22-28

"Jesus, help me please!" I screamed out with all
the air that I could muster. The pain was

overwhelming! This was an extreme shock to my system and to my ego. I had just fallen from the attic, and I could see the swelling of my leg through my boot. As I looked around the cold, damp garage, I felt lost. Yes, I was in my home, but I felt like, all of a sudden, God had forgotten me. I continued to yell as tears escaped their floodgates, and my pride left me faster than a prisoner leaving his cell for chow. I could barely move, and from the look of my injury, my leg was definitely broken. No one was coming! It was the middle of the day, and living in a working community, my neighbors were not home.

I was alone and sweating, and now fear was making an entrance to the center stage of this awful situation. "God, where are you?" I whispered through the pain, "You said that You would never leave me, and here I am, alone." This was a moment that I was not proud of. Just as quickly as I had been on top of the world, I was now laying in the bowels of pain, and my spirit was sinking fast. Had God finally left me? Is He upset at me for some reason? This was an uncomfortable and foreign feeling. "Calm down," I said to myself. As soon as I spoke these words, I saw a life raft for my sinking soul: my cell phone.

Esau Is Coming

I have always said that the greatest comedian in the universe is God. We constantly make plans with what we want to do with our lives, and I believe it makes God giggle. He is the master builder for all of His children's lives. How dare a finite creature make plans with a day that they did not create. Our majestic and wonderful God is in control at all times. There is never a time in history where God the Father has left His throne in heaven. We think we surprise God by our actions, but there is no jumping from behind a door to startle the King of Kings. God had everything in our lives mapped out before He even breathed into our delicate lungs. The *ruach* (breath) of God entered into mankind's nostrils knowing that the vessel was perfectly flawed. He does not violate our free will but knows each of our footprints before they make an impression in the sand.

For this reason alone, I am convinced that there are no accidents in life. God is the Master Architect. I have had to sit through countless funerals where a person crossed over from life unto death by accident. Please do not take it that I am in any way being disdainful or insolent. To the contrary, my heart is grieved at the pain of others. It simply saddens me more that some believe that God is not in control of the universe that He created. No one dies on accident. Life is not a series of random events, and God is not a mean kid sitting in heaven with a magnifying glass. Every single breath that we inhale and exhale has a divine purpose. This is good news when looked at from the proper perspective.

Let us examine for a minute the life of Jacob. He was a twin who had stolen the birthright of his older brother. Not only had he taken something that did not belong to him, but he stole it from a person who was skilled in the art of killing. His brother Esau was the hunter in the family. He spent most of his time killing animals, and shedding blood was no big deal to him. Jacob, on the other hand, was what some would call a momma's boy. His time was spent in the kitchen, and now he was facing a huge dilemma: Esau was coming. Not only was his older brother coming, but in the last conversation they had, Esau had promised to kill his little brother (Genesis 27:41). This is dysfunction at its finest. Aren't you happy that your family is not the only one with its share of issues?

All these years passed. Jacob had two wives, several children, and livestock, and he was considered a very blessed person. But Esau was coming! It is a difficult thing when your past is having a head-on collision with your present. I believe many of us can relate to this predicament. It is a hard thing to deal with when everything that you have been running from finally catches up with you. It is not because you got winded or were gasping for air—the speed of the past is unfathomable. No matter the speed of your retreat, it seems to always catch up with you when you least expect it.

Imagine that you have met the woman of your dreams. You are in love for the first time in your life. You get down on one knee, propose, and she readily accepts your love. Life could not get any better than this. All your life you have traveled from bed to bed looking for happiness that didn't exist in sinful acts. Now, God has given you a ray of sunshine in a heart that was accustomed to being gloomy. You go home feeling like you can conquer the world, until there is a knock on the door. A sheriff serves you with child support papers for twins that you did not know even existed. You are now a new father, and to make things worse, the babies are from a woman that you had to put a restraining order on for breaking out your car windows. This may seem far-fetched to some but close to reality for others. The Apostle Paul said it best:

> *Do not be deceived, God is not mocked; for whatever a man sows, that he will also reap.*
>
> Galatians 6:7 (NKJV)

Life is sometimes a revolving door. I can recall my grandfather's wise words when he would say, "Be careful of the bridges that you burn." He said that you never know when you may have to cross that bridge again. Those words of wisdom are often echoed in my mind when I want to repay a person for a harm that they have caused me. It is a process, but I believe we as a community have to be careful of the seeds of negativity that we plant. Just like Jacob, we don't want to find ourselves in a pasture of blessings only to have the buzzards of the past threatening to pluck us out at any given moment.

Alone

The human spirit is a wonderful and strange thing. It is sometimes difficult to comprehend because of its complexity. There are times when it needs to be left alone in order to recharge itself. There are other times when it craves attention, like a newborn baby, in order to feel fulfilled. But there is no normal human being who likes to be alone for a great period of time. Even in America's penal system, the powers at be will place a prisoner in solitary confinement in order to correct unwanted behavior. While these inmates may have terrorized their peers, the very threat of being alone for great lengths of time tames the beast that would have normally been wild and uncooperative.

But here, we are able to get a glimpse on one of the greatest battles recorded in the sacred scriptures. Jacob is now a fighter! Wait a minute—Jacob is a fighter? For the uninformed, Jacob was never seen as a person who was a threat to anyone. His twin brother Esau was the one who was looked at as a warrior; but Jacob *is* a fighter. It is amazing when God allows you to be placed in different situations, you truly find out what you are made of. This man was always in the company of others. Even while his body was developing and blossoming in his mother's womb, Jacob was not alone. His brother Esau decided to make a break for daylight, and Jacob decided to grab on to his heel, because being alone was not part of Jacob's DNA.

> *The time came for her to give birth, and she had twin sons. The first one was reddish, and his skin was like a hairy robe, so he was named Esau. The second one was born holding on tightly to the heel of Esau, so he was named Jacob. Isaac was sixty years old when they were born.*
>
> Genesis 25:24-26 (GNT)

This momma's boy is alone. He was left alone in order to find out who he was. Too many times we feel like being in a crowd will help us to find our identity. This is not true at all. It is in the quiet times of reflection and deep thought that a person will find out who they are. A wise person once said, "You may be planted in a circle, but you will only grow outside the box." Jacob was learning this lesson quickly because he had temporarily emptied his nest, and now a stranger was attacking with full intensity. There was no warning that danger was on the horizon, but there are times in life when we have to struggle to move to the next level.

This unknown man attacked God's chosen vessel. This is good news to some and depressing to others. Many have been made to believe that once you are saved and in the bosom of God, life will be a bed of roses. This is not only untrue but also comical in a way. If Jesus had to suffer while He was on this earth, it would be selfish to think that we as children of the King of Kings would leave this earth without any pitfalls. Life is full of pain and heartaches, and at times we will have to fight not just in a spiritual sense, but also in a very physical way. You are going to have to put on your gloves if you want to receive your crown. Please understand that it is normal to not want to have confrontation, but this is not the reality of being a Christian. The Word of God is filled with different occasions where people had to engage in battle—oftentimes with people whom they once loved.

The King James Version of this text says that Jacob was "left alone." This is an indication that this whole encounter was a setup of some kind. He was expecting to fight with his brother, but the attack came from an unknown person. This antagonist came into Jacob's life without any warning. It is amazing that you can be living your life and then one day you are fighting battles that you never anticipated. You go to the mailbox, check your inbox on social media, or get a phone call, and all of a sudden your life is changed. This is why we must always be on guard and make prayer an important part of our lives. I believe that every Christian must have a pre-pray attitude. This simply means that even if there are no storms in your life, pray anyway. Most people keep an umbrella in their car just in case the clouds around them get dark. This is the same concept that we must have about prayer. Life will get dark. Life will have its fair share of storms, and we must protect ourselves at all times.

No Rules in a Fight

Before a boxer enters a ring to fight in a match, the rules have already been explained to them. I know you are saying to yourself, "But the referee goes over the rules in the ring." Actually, before they sign the contract, the rules are already established. This is largely due to the fact that the warrior wants to know what he or she is walking into.

Wouldn't it be great if we as servants of the Most High God knew all of the details that it took for God to create His special edifice in us? We would already know that the devil could not attack us when we are going through certain situations. Let's say, for instance, we were having a bad day, but the rules of engagement said that the adversary could not bother us. That would be great! But we know that this is not the case—at all! As a matter of fact, it seems that the enemy attacks with more venom when we are down and out. This is because there are no rules to this. Sure, God puts handcuffs on the enemy to control how much he can do to us, but the attack can still be brutal at times.

> *"Did you notice my servant Job?" the Lord asked. "There is no one on earth as faithful and good as he is. He worships me and is careful not to do anything evil. You persuaded me to let you attack him for no reason at all, but Job is still as faithful as ever." Satan replied, "A person will give up everything in order to stay alive. But now suppose you hurt his body—he will curse you to your face!" So the Lord said to Satan, "All right, he is in your power, but you are not to kill him." Then Satan left the Lord's presence and made sores break out all over Job's body.*
>
> Job 2:3-7

Job is a perfect example of being attacked for what seems like no reason. But as we continue to look closer at this battle that is in full swing, we realize something important. The enemy is ruthless. He is fighting Jacob, and when he sees that he is not winning, he cheats. He hits Jacob in his hip socket so hard some scholars believe it was dislocated. Wait for one minute! Jacob is not a skilled fighter, but he was on the verge of declaring victory in his first and only recorded fight. But the enemy did not care about rules or regulations. He was on the attack, and it all had a divine purpose. God was going to ultimately get the glory because of this battle.

We forget that God is aware of what is going on at all times. I can imagine God sitting ringside in this scuffle, sipping on some tea and waiting to bless this first-time warrior. In this skirmish, Jacob had given birth to a new him. He had pushed through a spiritual birth canal and did not know it. Yes, the attack was strong, but it was necessary. Just because you have to fight from time to time does not mean that God is not still in the blessing business. Oftentimes, it is in the fight that you will find your biggest blessings. It seems oxymoronic that pain will be the genesis to glory, but it's true.

Think for a second about a woman who is in labor. For hours, she is in dire pain and agony. The contractions have made her life a living hell, and she cannot wait for it to subside. No person in the room can truly understand what she is going through. Some mothers may be able to sympathize with her, but in this moment, she is the one baring the pain. Finally, the moment of truth arrives, the baby makes his grand entrance into the world, and the mother smiles. She actually takes the source of her pain, and she cuddles it without hesitation. This is symbolic of moving through the pain and heartache of life as we know it. We have to know that sooner or later the pain will be over, and we are going to receive our blessings. Yes, the attack was sudden. Yes, the attack left us limping and at times feeling like God had abandoned us. But the end result is glory to God and the enemy knows that he has to fight you every time he comes your way.

When I was young, there was a kid that used to pick on me almost every day. It came to a point that I almost hated going to school because I knew that I had to see him eventually. My upbringing was one where if we got into trouble at school, my mother would deal with us with the heat of some leather on our backside.

So one day, my uncle came over, and I asked him what I should do. He first asked me if I was afraid of this kid. When I assured him that I wasn't, he gave me the best advice ever. He said, when the bully came my way, fight him without hesitation! I gladly took his advice, and not only did I win the fight with ease, but we later became friends. Please understand—I am not advocating violence towards anyone. What I am saying is there has to come a time when you have to put the fear into your adversary.

When you wake up in the morning, the gates of hell should tremble because God has allowed you one more day! The enemies of heaven should be fearful of your presence when he is attacking your friends and family. You should affect and infect all that comes into your presence by the power of God that is with you every day. How, you ask? By fighting for YOUR LIFE! We only live once, and you have to make the most out of it. Do not allow depression, your past, your insecurities, or even your family to stop you from getting all that the Lord has for you.

This battle became a blessing for Jacob, but only because he fought the good fight. He could have cried and complained. He could have begged for mercy. He could have taken a thousand different avenues to run from the fight, but he didn't. He fought! The Apostle Paul experienced a similar victory when he was at a point of death. He was proud that he didn't just lay down and get walked on:

> *For I am already being poured out as a drink offering, and the time of my departure is at hand. I have fought the good fight, I have finished the race, I have kept the faith. Finally, there is laid up for me the crown of righteousness, which the Lord, the righteous Judge, will give to me on that Day, and not to me only but also to all who have loved His appearing.*
>
> 2 Timothy 4:6-8 (NKJV)

BUILDING BLOCKS

Ask yourself these important questions:

1. What are you willing to fight for?

    _____

    _____

    _____

2. Do you feel like going into battle is a waste of time?

    _____

    _____

3. Does what you are fighting for bring you closer to God?

    _____

    _____

    _____

4. If it brings you closer to God, why are you stalling?

_____

_____

_____

5. What is the last thing you fought for?

_____

_____

_____

6. Does the enemy know your name?

_____

7. Do you feel like you are a warrior or a wimp for the kingdom?

_____

_____

◆ ◆ ◆ ◆ ◆ ◆ ◆ ◆ Conclusion ◆ ◆ ◆ ◆ ◆ ◆ ◆ ◆

To the beautiful person that is reading this book, I want you to know that you are not only important to God, but you are also wanted.

It may be strange to see this at first because you have to leave your area of comfort. Understand that God is the architect of your life, and He is constructing an amazing human being. Do not allow anyone to downgrade you because of your mistakes—it is part of the process. Stay focused and do not expose your blueprints to the enemy. One of the most valuable tools that you have in your tool belt is becoming naked before God. This is going to be one of your greatest assets in growth because God wants all of you. He does not want to date. He desires to be married to you.

Finally, get ready to fight for your life. The victory is already declared in heaven, but we must fight small battles while living on this planet. Remember that each experience is just another brick in the wonderful edifice that God is erecting. You are becoming something that others will admire for years to come. Know that God loves you, and in His eyes, you are a beautiful edifice.

◆◆◆◆◆◆◆ About the Author ◆◆◆◆◆◆◆

Ray Sorrell is a comedian, motivational speaker and the founder of CantGetRight Ministries, where comedy is used as a major teaching tool to reach God's people.

His stage name, CantGetRight, was developed because no one can "get right" without the help of God. He has been a licensed minister for almost twenty years and has a degree in social work from Our Lady of the Lake University. Currently, he is working on his Masters in Divinity from Wayland Baptist University. A well sought-after Christian comedian, Ray has a heart for people who are lost and a passion to help others see how much God loves them. His motto is, "The only time you should look down on a person is if you are helping them up."

Ray currently resides in San Antonio, Texas. Along with being a comedian, Ray loves reading, riding motorcycles, traveling, working with the youth in his community, and spending time with his three children: Savannah, Domunique, and Imani. Book Ray to speak at your event, email Made2serve70@gmail.com.

♦ ♦ ♦ ♦ ♦ ♦ ♦ ♦ ♦ ♦ Sources ♦ ♦ ♦ ♦ ♦ ♦ ♦ ♦ ♦ ♦

WE WANT TO HEAR FROM YOU!!!

If this book has made a difference in your life Ray would be delighted to hear about it.

LEAVE A REVIEW ON AMAZON.COM!

FOLLOW RAY ON SOCIAL MEDIA

Facebook: Comedian Ray-CANTGETRIGHT-Sorrell

Instagram & Twitter: @CANT1GETRIGHT

YouTube: CantGetRight

"EMPOWERING YOU TO IMPACT GENERATIONS"
WWW.PUBLISHYOURGIFT.COM

CPSIA information can be obtained
at www.ICGtesting.com
Printed in the USA
FSOW02n1508160517
34099FS